Coloring book for adults and kids amazing wolf image for design

This coloring book is belongs to

____

____

____

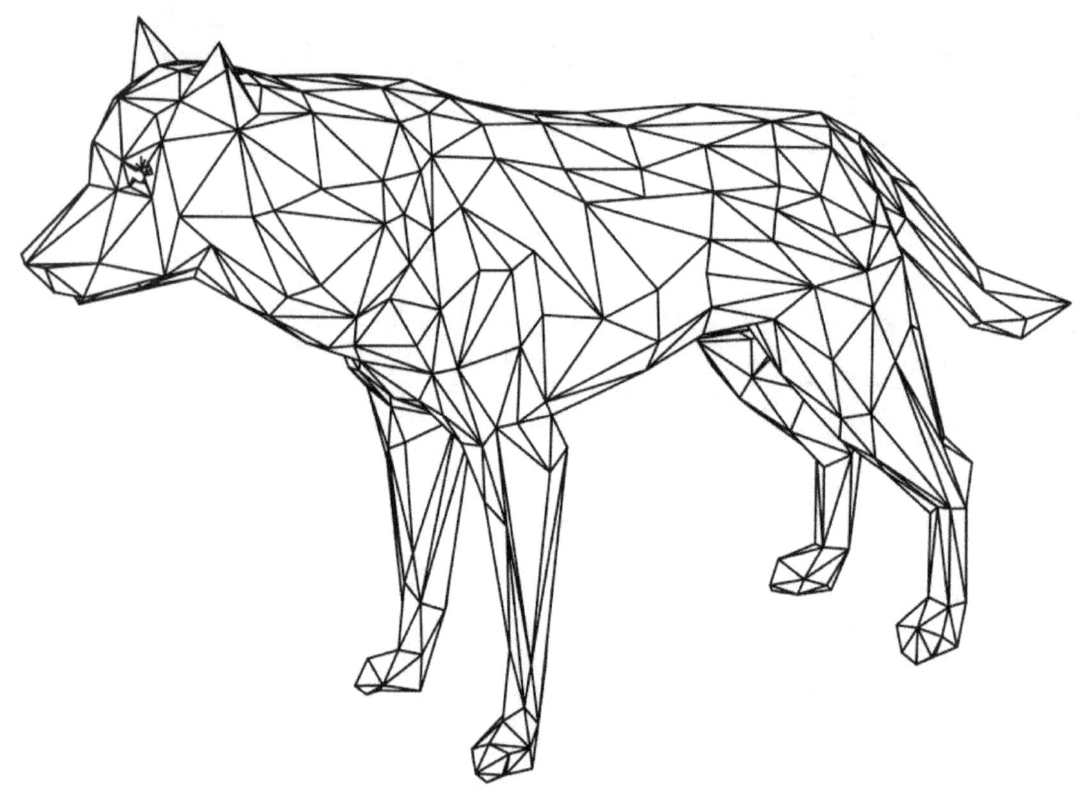

WOLF
SAMPLE LOCATION

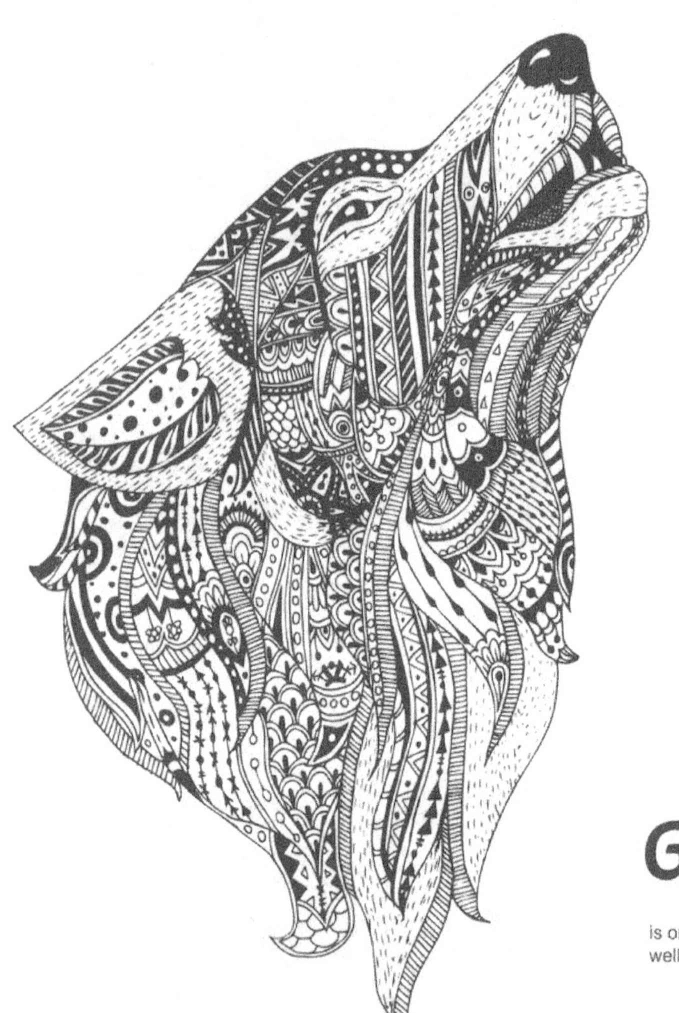

Gray wolf

is one of the world's best known and
well researched animals

Gray wolf

is one of the world's best known and
well researched animals

WOLF

狼